nage Information Series

About Drinking

Th
ren
be

Re
ha
s

All about Drinking
Dr Elizabeth McCall Smith is a general medical practitioner in Edinburgh.
Dr Alexander McCall Smith is the author of a number of books on medico-legal matters.

Teenage Information Series

All About Drinking

Elizabeth and Alexander McCall Smith

Chambers

First published by Macdonald Publishers Edinburgh
This edition published by W & R Chambers Ltd Edinburgh 1986
Reprinted 1987

British Library Cataloguing in Publication Data

McCall Smith, Elizabeth
    All about drinking. — Rev. ed. —
    (Teenage information series)
    1. Alcoholism   2. Youth — Alcohol use
    I. Title   II. McCall Smith, Alexander
    III. Series
    613.8'1   RC565

ISBN 0 550 20563 2
ISBN 0 550 75216 1 student ed.

Illustrations by Hazel McGlashan

Printing and Binding by Eyre & Spottiswoode Ltd, London and Margate

Contents

1. Talking about Alcohol

'Have a drink?'

That's quite a common thing to hear today. You've probably heard it at home or at parties. You've certainly heard it on television. Everywhere you look, people seem to be drinking. There are advertisements showing them drinking, and in just about every street there are shops selling alcohol.

If you look at the figures which tell us how much alcohol is being drunk, you'll see a similar picture. People seem to be drinking more and more, and the problems which drinking brings seem to be getting bigger and bigger. It is very difficult to say why this should be so, but one opinion is that it is because modern life has lots of stresses and strains that are making people drink too much in an effort to relax and cope.

Because there's a lot said about drinking and because there's so much alcohol about, it's quite important that we should know just what alcohol is and how it affects us. Knowing about alcohol is the best way of being able to keep a sensible attitude towards it.

In this book we don't say that you should never touch alcohol. What we do say is that you must be very careful when you're dealing with alcohol. The younger you are, the more careful you must be. You may not use alcohol at the moment, but you should still know about it, as you may have friends who drink it and they may encourage you to drink as well.

If you have already started to drink alcohol, you may find this book helpful as it may give you information you have not had access to before.

2. Types of Drink

Any liquid which you can drink can, of course, be called a 'drink', but what we're talking about here are alcoholic drinks. They are called alcoholic because they contain the drug ethanol, commonly called *alcohol*.

Some drinks do not contain alcohol. These non-alcoholic drinks are, by and large, harmless. Tea and coffee, for example, are non-alcoholic drinks, but they do contain small amounts of a substance called *caffeine*, which can have an effect on the body.

However, alcoholic drinks are quite different from all other kinds of drinks. The alcohol they contain has an effect which is far more serious than, say, the effect of sugar in Coke, or caffeine in coffee.

What is alcohol?

Often people use the word 'alcohol' to talk about all sorts of alcoholic drinks. Beer, whisky and wine are all very different drinks but all may be described as alcohol. Of course, alcohol is just one of the things which these alcoholic drinks contain. It is, however, the active part of them, the part that has the real effect.

A glass of beer consists of a lot of water, some other substances, and a smallish amount of actual alcohol.

Alcohol is a clear, colourless liquid with a very sharp taste. It is formed when a chemical process called *fermentation* takes place. Fermentation occurs when yeast is added to sugar solutions. Yeast changes sugar into alcohol and the gas carbon dioxide.

Different drinks contain different amounts of alcohol. Strong drinks, such as whisky or brandy, contain more alcohol than weaker drinks such as beer or cider. The table below is a guide to roughly how much alcohol various drinks contain.

BEER (Ale or Lager)

3.5% alcohol. This means that in every hundred parts, there will be about three and a half parts of alcohol. Some beers, of course, may be stronger, and may contain up to five parts of alcohol in every hundred parts of beer. These beers or lagers are often called 'special brews' or 'extra strong'.

WINE

11% alcohol. Wine is therefore about three times as strong as beer. One glass of wine contains as much alcohol as three of the same size glass of beer.

WHISKY, BRANDY, GIN

These drinks contain around 40% alcohol. They are much stronger than beer or wine — about ten times as strong as beer and about four times as strong as wine.

The various sorts of alcoholic drink

There are three main sorts of alcoholic drink; beer, wine, spirits. They are made in different ways and from different substances, and, as we have just seen, they contain different amounts of alcohol.

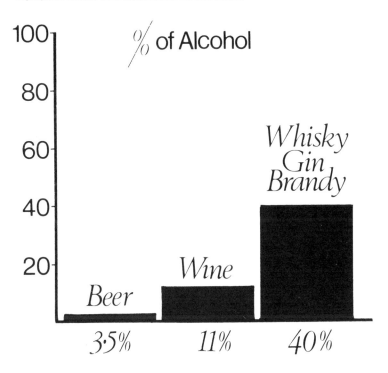

BEER (Ale or Lager)

This is one of the most popular drinks in many countries. It is readily available and will often be the main social drink as it is relatively inexpensive. For many people, beer is the first alcoholic drink they try.

Beer is made from barley, which is a type of grain, and from hops and sugar. It is made in breweries where the ingredients are allowed to ferment in vast vats. By adding yeast to the mixture, alcohol is produced, and the resulting liquid is then bottled or put into cans. In bars, beer may be served from large barrels, or casks, which are connected to taps.

Beer often tastes quite bitter, but it is a refreshing drink to those who have developed a taste for it.

WINE

Wine can be red, white, or rosy-coloured. White wine is not really white — it is often golden-coloured or even slightly green.

Wines that you see in shops are produced from grapes, though people who make their own wine at home may make it from other things. Almost all fruit and many vegetables can be used to make wine.

To make a wine

The juice from the grapes is allowed to ferment and produce alcohol. It is then left in kegs or casks while it matures—often it is left for many years. It may on the other hand be bottled almost immediately. If wine is drunk before it is ready (mature), it can have an acid or bitter taste. This is why you often hear people discussing the *age* of a wine. In the case of some wines, the older they are, the better they taste.

Some people make a big thing about wine, talking about where it came from, who made it, what it tastes like, etc. It is true that with more expensive wines these things affect taste and enjoyment; however, with many less expensive wines these factors matter very little.

SPIRITS

Spirits are produced by the process of distillation. This involves boiling off the alcohol in fermented liquid and using the alcohol collected in this way to produce a drink which is stronger in alcohol.

Spirits are made from a variety of substances, though it is usually grain that is used. Whisky, for example, is made from barley or from rye. Spirits can be colourless (like gin and vodka) or they may have a darkish colour (whisky is a golden-brown colour and certain types of rum are dark brown).

Are there other drinks apart from these?

There are many other sorts of drinks available. If you look at the shelves in a bar, you will see bottle after bottle of strange-looking liquids, many of them with names few people have ever heard of. Many of these drinks are *liqueurs*, which are spirits to which certain extra ingredients have been added. Although liqueurs often have a scented or spicy odour, and quite a sweet taste, they are very strong.

Another common drink is *cider*, which is produced from apples. Ciders may be quite weak, but don't be fooled — some are very strong.

Sherry and *port* are wines to which further alcohol has been added.

What is a cocktail?

A cocktail is a mixture of drinks which is sometimes called by a rather fancy name. Usually these mixtures contain spirits of some sort. Sometimes they contain non-alcoholic drinks as well, or even pieces of fruit, but because they contain spirits, often mixed spirits, cocktails are usually strong drinks.

Punch and fruit cup

Sometimes at parties a mixed drink is served from a large container. This drink may have fruit floating about in it and may be quite sweet to the taste. It is usually called punch or fruit cup.

Drinks of this sort may be stronger than you suspect, as they may contain spirits such as rum or brandy.

3. What Alcohol Does

When a person has an alcoholic drink, the body begins to absorb the alcohol when it enters the mouth. It then goes down to the stomach where some alcohol passes through the stomach lining and into the bloodstream. The rest leaves the stomach and enters the small intestine, from which it is absorbed into the bloodstream more rapidly. Via the bloodstream it reaches the brain where it has its main effect.

How quickly does alcohol get into the blood?

Alcohol doesn't go straight into the blood—it usually takes a few minutes for the body to absorb it. This is why it is a little while before you feel the effect of a drink.

How quickly alcohol gets into the blood depends on a number of things. These are:

—*How quickly alcohol is drunk.* A person who takes a number of drinks quickly will have more alcohol in their blood than somebody who takes the same number of drinks more slowly.

—*The dilution, amount and type of drink.* Generally alcohol diluted with water or a soft drink will get into the bloodstream more slowly than undiluted alcoholic drink.

—*Whether or not the person taking the drink has eaten anything.* If there is food in the stomach, the alcohol will be taken into the bloodstream more slowly.

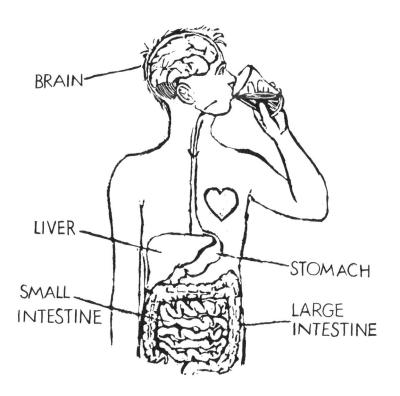

Carol and Sue

Carol and her friend Sue went to a party where cider was being given to the guests. Neither of them had drunk much before and neither of them knew much about drink.

Carol was given a cider and sipped at it while she was talking to a boy she knew from school. The person giving the party had made some sandwiches, so she ate some of these while she talked and drank her cider.

Sue didn't eat anything. She drank her first cider quickly and had another one shortly after that. On her third cider she felt quite light-headed and slightly sick. She could not carry on a conversation and certainly didn't feel like dancing. She was drunk and was certainly not enjoying herself. Nor was she of any use to her friends. She was making a complete fool of herself and was aware of that as well.

Carol also drank three ciders that night, but she drank them more slowly. She also ate while she drank. She did not get drunk and didn't make a fool of herself.

Why? Sue had a lot of alcohol in her blood because of the way she drank the cider. Carol had a smaller amount of alcohol in her blood because she had drunk the cider slowly and more sensibly. It makes a difference how you drink, as well as how much you drink.

How does alcohol affect you?

Alcohol is a drug. It's different from the sort of drugs that often make the headlines in newspapers—dope, heroin, LSD and so on—because the effect it has on you is different, and it is not against the law to use it in most countries. Like most drugs, other than those that your doctor gives you when you're ill, alcohol changes the way you feel. It changes your mood and it may affect the way you talk or move.

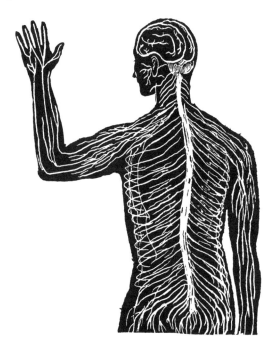

Alcohol does this by acting on the brain. Its action on the brain is to *depress the central nervous system*. This means that alcohol mixes up certain things which the brain and the nervous system normally do, like controlling your behaviour and physical co-ordination. It has an effect on your power to judge things and your power to control your arms and legs.

Here's what may happen after you've had alcohol:

—You may begin to feel elated or act as if you're very happy. You may say things which you wouldn't normally say. You may feel like doing something you'd normally feel too shy to do.

—You may not be able to judge distances correctly. The way you see things may be a bit confused.

—Your reactions may be slowed down. It may take you a bit of time to react to something that somebody says or does. For example, if somebody threw you a ball, you might fumble or be too slow to catch it.

—On the other hand, you may begin to feel sad or depressed.

To give you an idea of the way alcohol works, the following pictures tell you the effects that various amounts of alcohol usually have.

1 Drink

You feel a bit 'high'. You may feel warm and happy or even depressed.

2 Drinks

You may feel a bit drowsy. Your judgement may be mixed up.

13

3-4 Drinks

Your judgement now becomes badly mixed up. You can't speak properly. You may not be able to control the way you walk.

5 or More

You may not understand what is being said to you. You may actually not be able to stand up. You may even become very ill; perhaps even lose consciousness.

The reactions illustrated are very rough. People react to alcohol in different ways: some can drink several drinks without being badly affected by it, others are affected badly by just one or two drinks. If you do drink, you should know what your 'limit' is. In other words, you should know how many drinks you can take without getting drunk.

When does a person become drunk?

If you have one drink and feel a bit warm and happy as a result, that does not mean that you're drunk. We only say that people are drunk when they've had a lot of alcohol and are obviously not in control of themselves. If they are losing control of their legs or their behaviour, if they are shouting or laughing in a strange way, then they may be drunk.

Some people who have had too much alcohol may become quiet. As I have already mentioned, some people find that alcohol makes them feel sad or miserable. They may not become talkative or excited, but may simply lapse into a state of depression.

Does alcohol make people want to fight?

Not everybody who drinks alcohol feels like going out straight away and picking a fight. Some people do, however, and it is better if people who are affected in this way keep away from alcohol. If you find that alcohol makes you feel like fighting, then you will have to be very careful. A lot of people do things when they are drunk which they would never dream of doing when they are sober. It's all very well saying afterwards, 'I only did it because I was drunk': the judge might say, 'Well, you shouldn't have got drunk in the first place!' At the very least such anti-social behaviour can cost you friends and a normal social life.

Sobering up and hangovers

Once the alcohol is in your bloodstream, there is nothing that you can do to get it out again. All that you can do is wait for your body to get rid of it. The speed with which this happens depends on how much alcohol there is in the body to start with. The body can only deal with a certain amount at a time. There is no other way to become sober except by waiting. It is not true that black coffee sobers you up.

What is a hangover?

Colin woke up on Sunday morning with a head that felt as though it was going to split in two.

15

He had been to a party the night before and had had too much to drink. He had arrived home drunk and had fallen into bed with half his clothes still on. He had had a good time at the party, but now he was beginning to regret it.

He really did feel ill. The taste in his mouth was like nothing he had ever tasted before—almost as if he had gargled with vinegar, and his head throbbed and throbbed. He had a hangover.

If you drink too much, it is not unusual to feel very ill the next day. There is no cure for it. Having another drink does not cure it, as some people seem to think.

Hangovers are caused by the accumulation of certain substances in the body's tissues as well as by the way that alcohol acts on the brain. A person with a hangover also feels sick in the stomach. This is usually caused by the alcohol irritating the stomach lining.

Alcohol also acts on the kidneys, making you pass more water; your body becomes dehydrated and this too contributes to your feeling unwell.

As with most things for which there is no cure, the best answer is to avoid having a hangover at all. Never drink too much and you'll never have a hangover. It's that simple! However, you can reduce some of the unpleasant effects of a hangover by gentle rehydration of your body with regular small drinks of water and fruit juice, which will replace lost salts and vitamins.

Why do people drink?

People have all sorts of reasons for explaining why they like to drink alcohol. Here are some of the most common ones:

It makes me feel good.
Alcohol can make people feel elated. As we have already seen, when you've had one or two drinks you may feel warm and pleasant—you may feel more cheerful.

Alcohol may also make you feel physically relaxed. If you are tense or tired, alcohol may have the effect of making you feel better. Drinking for relaxation is a major reason why people may have a drink at the end of a hard day.

I drink because it helps me to get on with people.
Alcohol can make you feel relaxed and at ease, so some people say that they find it easier to get on with people if they've had a drink. Alcohol may make it easier for them to talk to their friends and they may think that they are better company. (This is, of course, not always true. Certainly, when people have had more than a small amount of alcohol, they are not good company at all).

I drink to get away from my problems.
Sadly, there are people who drink in order to get away from problems. Alcohol may help them to forget the things that are bothering them, but problems don't disappear with drink. In fact they may increase with drinking, and drinking itself may become one of them. This is an unhealthy and even dangerous reason to drink.

Habit.
Some people drink because they have formed a habit of drinking. This too is very dangerous, as we'll see in the section of this book that deals with alcoholism. Alcohol is *addictive* both physically and psychologically (emotionally)—that is, it can get a hold of you and you may always want to have one drink after another.

I drink because everybody else does.
Doing something because other people do it is often a bad idea, but it is true that this is why some people drink alcohol. The social pressures may be very strong and it takes self-confidence to turn down offered drinks when you are with other people who are drinking.

It is often considered 'manly' or 'sophisticated' to drink. It is interesting to note that the people we admire the most in society, the great thinkers, artists, athletes and businessmen, generally drink very rarely and often not at all, so that their minds and bodies are capable of handling great stress.

Michael

Michael was just 16. Shortly after his birthday he went to a party with some friends at the home of someone whose parents were away. There was quite a lot of beer around, and Michael and his friends were given a few bottles each.

Michael had not drunk before. He had had sips of wine now and then and had been given a few swigs of beer by his father. But that was all.

Michael's friends had all drunk before. They drank their beers quickly. Michael found that he didn't like the taste of beer and also found that it didn't make him feel particularly good. His friends all urged him to drink and some of them even laughed at him when they saw how slowly he was drinking.

In order not to be thought any different from them, Michael drank the beer quickly. When the others had another bottle he did too, although he was not particularly enjoying himself.

Soon he felt ill. He was dizzy and couldn't think straight. Michael had not wanted to drink so much. What made him keep drinking? Was Michael's condition the result of choice, or pressure from his friends? What should Michael have done to avoid this situation?

4. What Can Go Wrong?

We've seen that drinking alcohol can have some effects on you that are quite pleasant—as long as you don't drink too much. For this reason many people take the occasional drink and do not really suffer very much harm from it. But there are people who are very badly harmed by alcohol. These are people who become very heavy drinkers and who may one day become *alcoholics*. Alcoholics have a major problem and may eventually die from drinking too much. Certainly alcoholism puts a major strain on an alcoholic's relationships with family and friends.

So we must separate two sorts of drinking. One sort of drinking is called *social drinking*. The other sort is sometimes called *problem drinking*.

What is social drinking?

When people only drink now and then, and only in company, it is usually defined as social drinking. For example, a person may go round for a meal at somebody else's house. When they arrive, they may be offered a drink of some sort, and there may be wine served with the meal. If nobody drinks very heavily, and the conversation and atmosphere are not harmed by the drink, then that is social drinking. Alcohol is just part of the evening's social activities— like the conversation, or the food.

Here is the sort of drinking that a normal social drinker may do:

Gill works in an office. On Friday evening the people she works with go off to a bar and have a drink. Gill goes with them and has a drink or two while they all sit around and chat. Everyone is in a good mood as it is the end of the week. After Gill has had a couple of drinks she goes home for dinner.

On Saturday, Gill goes to a party. There is wine at this party, and she drinks three glasses over the evening. Somebody offers her a large glass of brandy, but she turns it down. She is not interested in getting drunk.

Gill is a typical social drinker. If that is all she drinks each week, then drinking is no problem for her. She only drinks when she is with other people and she does not drink too much.

Heavy drinking

Unlike Gill, Tom is a heavy drinker. Every evening after work he goes into a bar and orders himself a large whisky. Then, when he has finished this, he orders another. When he goes home, he may have more to drink, even if there is nobody else there. Most nights he has too much to drink. At weekends he drinks during the day. Tom finds that he *needs* alcohol, that he *has to have a drink*.

Tom usually has a few drinks before he goes to a party ('just to get into the mood') and then when he arrives he drinks very quickly. He's not all that interested in talking to people—all he wants to do is to drink as much alcohol as he can, in as short a time as possible.

What is an alcoholic?

Tom, the heavy drinker we have just described, is probably an alcoholic. This means that he has got himself into a position where he has to have a drink. His body has become accustomed to alcohol and it craves it all the time. Tom is hooked on alcohol.

Just about anybody who drinks *could* become an alcoholic. The person who drinks must always be ready to ask himself or herself these questions:

Am I drinking too much?

Is drinking beginning to change my life?

Could I stop drinking if I wanted to?

Drinking too much

People can start becoming alcoholics when they begin to drink more than other social drinkers. The quantity of alcohol that you drink is the important thing here. If you usually drink three beers rather than just drinking one, then the risk of your becoming an alcoholic is much greater.

Another thing to be careful about is drinking too often. The more often you drink, the more your mind and body become used to having alcohol. As a result of this, you would begin to want to have a drink every evening.

When drinking changes your life

This is another danger signal. When drink begins to change the way a person behaves, then it is clear that there is something going wrong, and that he or she may be in danger of becoming an alcoholic. A person with a drink problem may begin to forget to do the things he has to do, or he may just not feel like doing them any more. Some young people who drink find that they begin to miss school, or that they begin to get into trouble with their parents or the police.

If you begin to think too much about drinking, then you are in danger of building up a drink problem for yourself. People with drink problems often think of nothing else but getting drunk. They may talk about drinking a lot of the time, which makes them rather boring for their friends. Soon most of the people they spend any time with are those who also have drinking problems.

Stopping drinking

If somebody finds it hard to stop drinking, then they certainly have a drink problem. In many ways, drinking is like smoking: it's not hard to start it, but giving it up can be harder than you think.

It is very difficult to give up drinking once you have become a heavy drinker. Many heavy drinkers feel unable to face life without alcohol.

The body also becomes used to drink, and begins to need the alcohol that it has come to expect. So, both physically and emotionally, drink becomes a need.

People who have become alcoholics find it very difficult to get back to an ordinary life again. Often they refuse to accept that they have a drink problem, and they may use all sorts of tricks to hide their drinking from other people. They will even lie to themselves as to the amount they drink and how often.

Sometimes people with an alcohol problem decide that they want to give up drink, and are able to do so without the help of others. They start to control their drinking, even though they find it very uncomfortable. They may manage to give up drink altogether. It is possible—with will power, and the sympathetic understanding of friends, family and professional people.

Doctors can help, sometimes by sending the drinker to a special clinic. There are also groups of people—such as Alcoholics Anonymous—who help the heavy drinker to return to an alcohol-free life. These people, who have usually had a bad drink problem themselves, help alcoholics by providing friendship and support. They show them what they have become through drinking too much, and then help them to fill their lives with other things. There are also groups to help the families of alcoholics, as it is often the families who really suffer when drinking gets out of control.

A drinking problem in your family?

As we have already mentioned, when somebody has a drinking problem, it is usually not just that person who suffers. Heavy drinking affects friends and family and often makes them just as unhappy as the person with the problem.

Alcoholics may allow drink to dominate their lives. They may forget about the feelings of the people who are close to them and they may not realise that the way they use alcohol is breaking up the family.

How do I know if somebody in my family is drinking too much?

In most cases, people who drink too much will give some sign of their problem by the way they behave. They may appear drunk in the house. They may become violent after they have had too much to drink, and there may be a lot of family fights.

On the other hand, heavy drinkers may try to hide the fact that they are drinking too much. Alcoholics sometimes conceal their bottles in hiding places, so that

25

the evidence of their drinking is not there for everyone to see.

If you have, for example, a father who is a heavy drinker, you will probably see some signs of this. His behaviour may be strange and he may go through odd moods. You will probably smell alcohol on his breath. There may be periods when he goes off by himself and becomes drunk. This may lead to disruption of family life. Meals may be broken up or may not be made. Things which have to be done may not get done. Your father's moods may change so quickly that you will sometimes not know where you stand.

What should I do if there is an alcoholic in the family?

If someone in your family has a drink problem, the most important thing to do is to work out a way of keeping life going as normally as possible. You must not think that alcoholics can change their ways quickly. You may have to live with the problem for a long time and the sooner you can come to terms with that the better, for you will have to try to cope with the problems that drinking presents.

Don't try to give lectures to your drinking parent. At the same time, there may be an occasion when it will be possible for you to talk to your parent about drinking. If this is possible, there is no reason why you shouldn't tell him or her what heavy drinking is doing to the family and how upset it makes you. This might help to convince the parent that it is time to seek out help.

You could consider joining Alateen, an organisation linked to Alcoholics Anonymous whose address you will find in the telephone directory.

Where to get help

If you are bullied or beaten by a drinking parent, there are ways of dealing with this. It is against the law for a parent to mistreat a child, and you can count on help from a number of people. It might be best to discuss it with relatives first, but if this does not help then you can speak to somebody else. A teacher may be able to help you or you may be able to get help from somebody else you trust, such as your family doctor.

5. Alcohol and Health

Although a small amount of alcohol will not harm your health, there is no doubt at all that drinking a lot of alcohol can damage the body in a number of serious ways. Here are some of the things that heavy drinking can do:

Alcohol can harm the liver

The liver is an organ in the body that helps to purify the blood in your veins. When alcohol is drunk and gets into the blood, it passes into the liver and there the process of changing the alcohol into other substances begins. Slowly, alcohol is changed by the body into water and a gas called carbon dioxide.

However, if too much alcohol is drunk over a long period of time, the liver can be badly damaged. A very serious disease, cirrhosis, can result from alcohol-damage to the liver, and many heavy drinkers die of this disease.

Drinking in moderation—that is, social drinking which is kept under control—will not usually cause real damage to the liver.

Is alcohol bad for the stomach?

Once again, the answer to this depends on the amount you drink. Somebody who drinks small amounts of alcohol will probably not damage their stomach. When too much is drunk, the lining of the stomach becomes irritated and inflamed and this can cause pain and bleeding. In some cases the lining may even perforate and this, of course, is a serious matter.

Can alcohol harm the brain?

Doctors have produced evidence that alcohol can damage the brain. A person who drinks too much may lose his memory. Over a long period his entire personality may change completely, and he may have to spend the rest of his life in an institution.

Drinking and pregnancy

Women who drink when expecting a baby may damage the health of the baby. Since the baby receives its blood and food from the mother while it is still in her womb, if there is alcohol in the mother's blood, the baby receives that too.

Drinking mothers sometimes give birth to babies whose heads are not normally formed. If the mother has drunk a great deal, then the baby may be slower to develop than other children.

Other ways in which alcohol is harmful

It is not unusual to find that people who drink too much harm their health by failing to look after themselves properly. Heavy drinkers often do not eat enough, and because of this their bodies suffer through malnutrition. They may damage themselves by falling over and hurting themselves when they are drunk. In some cases they may even suffocate in their own vomit. Ask any doctor who has served in an emergency ward and you will be told that many of the emergency cases are alcoholics who have injured themselves while under the influence of drink.

Remember—if you are very careful with alcohol, then none of these things is likely to happen to you. But you have to be *very* careful and you must be ready to act quickly if you begin to think that you are drinking too much.

Alcohol and the opposite sex

Sometimes you see advertisements which seem to say that if you drink a certain drink you'll have a great time and have plenty of friends of the opposite sex. Most of us know these advertisements are not true, but nevertheless advertising works in a subtle way and if we examine our motives we often find that we have been influenced by this false logic. Drinking alcohol has got nothing to do with having lots of friends. You have friends because of what you're like, not because of what you drink.

It's also wrong to think that you become more attractive when you're drunk. If you're a boy, ask any girl and she'll tell you that spending time with a boy who has drunk too much is not much fun for her. If you're a girl, any boy will tell you that the sight of a girl who has drunk too much is the biggest turn-off that he can imagine.

6. Drinking and the Law

It is not illegal to drink alcohol. There may be some sorts of drinking which will get you into trouble with the police (in some countries, drinking in a public place may be against the law, particularly if you are under a certain age), but in general it is not a crime to drink.

If other drugs are against the law, shouldn't alcohol be illegal too?

It may seem strange that, although drugs such as dope are illegal, alcohol is legal. Some people argue that alcohol does far more harm to many more people than dope does, and in some senses they may be right. Alcohol does a great deal of harm, but because it has always been used in our society, it is accepted. This may be unfair to people who like to use dope, but it has been shown that it is very difficult to make it illegal to drink alcohol. When this was tried in the United States, the trouble that was caused was hardly worth it—even to those who believed that alcohol is very harmful and wanted it to be against the law to drink it.

Is it a crime for me to drink alcohol if I am still a minor?

It is usually not a crime for a young person to drink alcohol at home or at somebody else's home, but this does not mean that it is possible for a young person to go out and buy alcohol. This is against the law, and it is also illegal for a person under a certain age (usually eighteen) to go into a bar and have a drink.

These laws are designed to make it difficult for young people to get hold of alcohol unless it is given to them at home. Sometimes they may seem to be a bit unfair (a seventeen-year-old may not be going to harm himself very much by buying one beer), but if they did not exist then many young people would find themselves drinking too much.

Drinking and driving

It is against the law to drive a car or a motor cycle after drinking more than the legal amount. If you do, you're going to be a danger to yourself and to others. Alcohol slows your reactions and may change the way you see things. Imagine trying to drive using only one hand and closing one eye—it would hardly be easy! Or imagine trying to drive when you're very, very tired. Your driving would obviously be dangerous.

So it is when people try to drive after having more than a small quantity of alcohol. They may drive on the wrong side of the road, or drive too fast. They may not see other road users coming until it's too late, and might even kill somebody.

Remember, the more inexperienced you are as a drinker and as a driver the more likely it is that even a small amount of alcohol will make you unsafe on the road. The skills needed to drive are impaired by any alcohol in the blood-stream. By the time your blood alcohol is at the legal limit of 80 mg% you will definitely be a danger.

Driving after drinking is a crime that may lead to the loss of your driving licence and, in some cases, a prison sentence. If you cause an accident as a result of your drunken driving, then this will make it even more serious. Then there is also the question of how you would feel if your bad driving caused somebody to lose their life or to be seriously injured. This may be the worst part—as David was to find out.

David

David had just passed his driving test when he borrowed his father's car one Saturday night. Driving was still something quite new to him, and he got a lot of fun out of it. He was not a bad driver, and his father trusted him to bring the car home in one piece.

David drove round to pick up his friends. Altogether there were four people in the car—David, his girlfriend Anne, his friend Rob and Rob's girlfriend Kate. They drove round for a while and then they went to a house where they knew there was going to be a party. When they arrived the party had already started. The music was loud and everybody seemed to be having a good time.

There was quite a lot of beer at the party. David knew that he would have to be careful if he was to drive back, but he thought that he would just have one or two beers, and that would be quite all right.

After the second beer (which seemed to go quite quickly) David found himself in a really good mood. He started a third beer and then a fourth. With all the fun of the party, he forgot about driving.

Kate had to be back at twelve and Rob asked David if they could go. David now remembered about the car. He wondered if he might be too drunk to drive, but because of the good mood he was in, he decided to go ahead anyway. If he didn't drive back, then he would get into trouble with his father for not bringing the car back. 'I've got no choice,' he said to himself. 'I'll just be extra careful.'

David began to drive. Rob and Kate were in the back

seat and were laughing over something that somebody had done at the party. Anne was fiddling with the switches on the radio trying to find a good station.

David blinked. He felt good inside, but he found it a bit difficult to deal with the traffic. There were cars coming from the other side of the road and their lights seemed very bright. Anne suddenly said something to him.

'Slow down, you're going too fast.'

David looked at the speedometer. Anne was right—he was going too fast. Putting his foot on the brake pedal, he began to press it down. There were lights in front of him, red lights, the back of a truck. David pushed hard on the brakes, but there was not enough room to stop. With a thud and a crumpling, David felt the car go into the truck. He felt himself going forward and he heard screaming. Then there was nothing.

David and Anne were very lucky. In spite of the fact that they had piled right into the back of the truck, they suffered only concussion and a few scratches and bruises. Rob was all right too. He wasn't even knocked unconscious by the impact. Kate wasn't so lucky. When the car hit the truck, she was catapulted forward into the front seat and actually ended up against the car's instrument panel. Her face was badly cut and she lost some teeth. She had to have stitches across her cheek and under her chin. When the stitches came out, she was very badly scarred.

Of course, it could have been much worse. Nobody was killed or crippled in the accident, but Kate would have to go through life with ugly scars across her face. David still sees her from time to time, and each time he sees her he is reminded of the fact that it was his stupidity that caused the accident.

If David had not driven after drinking, then it wouldn't have happened.

Of course there was one other consequence. The police were called to the accident and David was breathalysed and taken to the police station. A blood sample was taken and this was over the legal limit. In court he was fined and lost his driving licence, so now he has to walk everywhere. When he gets his licence back he will find it very hard to get car insurance; if he does get it, then it will cost him much more.

7. Saying No

There is no reason why you should drink alcohol if you don't want to. Many people prefer not to drink at all. These people (sometimes called teetotallers) are quite happy to go to parties or celebrations and have soft drinks, lemonade or fruit juice for example, rather than alcohol. They are usually people who know their own minds well and who have decided that alcohol is not for them. Sometimes they are people who have had a bad time with alcohol in the past. They may have been alcoholics who have decided that the only way back to health is by refusing to touch alcohol in any circumstances. Sometimes they have religious reasons for not drinking.

If you decide that you don't want to drink (or even if you decide that you only want to drink on very special occasions) you must be prepared for pressure that may be put on you to change your mind. People who drink themselves sometimes try to persuade others to drink as well. 'Go on,' they may say. 'Join me.'

Why they should say this may seem a bid odd. After all, why should anyone want to persuade others to do what they are doing themselves? Perhaps it's just that they want people to have a good time with them. Perhaps in some cases it's because they may feel a bit guilty about drinking. If everyone is doing something, then it's often much easier to put any doubts to the back of your mind.

Whatever the reason for this sort of pressure, there is absolutely no reason why you should have a drink if you don't want one. To help you refuse, here are some of the things you can say. They may just be excuses, but they may make it easier for you to say 'no' without being made to feel foolish or a spoil-sport.

No thanks, it makes me sick.
If somebody is pressing you to have a drink and seems unwilling to let you say 'no', then this may be a useful thing to say. Nobody is likely to push you to drink something which will make you ill.

No thanks, I've got to stay sober.
It may be helpful to be able to give some excuse such as

this if you want to avoid pressure to drink. You could also say something like, 'No thanks, I've got to go home soon.'

No thanks, I'm in training.
You could say you are in training to get fit for football, hockey, rugby, athletics, or other sports.

My parents will go crazy if they smell it on my breath.
This may be useful. All young people have these kinds of controls placed upon them and a good friend will not want to get you into trouble with your parents.

What if somebody forces a drink on me?

This can be difficult. If you are unlucky enough to be with people who force a drink into your hand and then expect you to drink it, it may be very difficult to avoid an argument. Naturally enough, you may feel too shy to make a fuss.

In such a case, one way out of the problem is to accept the drink and to begin drinking it. You could just take a sip, so that the pressure is taken off you. Later on, it may be possible to get rid of the drink in a way which nobody will notice. On the other hand, you could just hold on to it but drink hardly any of it. This is a system followed by many people who have to go to parties and functions because of their job. They obviously will not want to drink at all of these, and so they may just hold their drink in their hand, always keeping it just about full by taking only small sips. In this way, people don't keep coming back to fill up their glasses.

There is *nothing weak* about not drinking. A non-drinker is not a spoil-sport or a coward: he or she is just somebody who prefers not to drink alcohol. Nobody laughs at people who don't like onions or anchovies— why should they laugh at somebody who doesn't like alcohol?

8. Final Points

- Nobody *has* to drink. If you decide that you are not going to drink at all, that's a good decision and many people will admire you for it. Ignore anybody who criticises you for it.

- If you do drink, always remember that alcohol can be very dangerous. Drink only a small amount, and you will be all right. Never drink too much as you may make a fool of yourself and you may cause harm to yourself and to others.

- Only drink when you are in company. Don't drink to get away from problems or because you are feeling low.

- Remember that drinking is not going to make you stronger, smarter, or more attractive. Drinking is not tough or clever.

- You don't have to drink to have a good time.